South Kest

on old picture posi̇cai u̇

Andrew Jenkins

1. Stamford - Town Bridge. The best way to enter Lincolnshire is northwards on the Great North Road through Stamford. This ancient route followed by the Roman Ermine Street, enters the county over the Town Bridge and runs up the west side of South Kesteven. In this view from around 1912, the George Hotel is to the left and St. Mary's Church crowns the hill beyond. Dolby Bros. of Stamford published the postcard.

Designed and published by
Reflections of a Bygone Age,
Keyworth, Nottingham 2004

Printed by Adlard Print &
Reprographics Ltd, Ruddington

£3.50

Introduction

This book has been conceived as a tour around the South Kesteven district of Lincolnshire, illustrated by postcards from the early part of the last century. As well as providing a glimpse of life in the area almost a hundred years ago, the book presents an unusual guide to a picturesque part of the country often missed by travellers passing by on the Great North Road (A1).

Kesteven is one of three ancient administrative divisions of Lincolnshire, the others being Lindsey and Holland. In more recent times it was split into North and South Kesteven. The southern district includes the market towns of Stamford, Bourne and Grantham, and is an area of limestone uplands and valleys, abundant woodland and mellow stone villages. It has long been noted as a pleasant place to live as witnessed by the many large estates and country houses in the area including Casewick in the south, Grimsthorpe near Bourne, and Belton near Grantham. Unspoilt by heavy industry, agriculture has always been the main source of income. Originally famed for sheep rearing, much of the area has now been turned over to arable crops.

South Kesteven also has strong historical connections. Hereward the Wake held lands near Witham-on-the-Hill and Colsterworth was the birthplace of Sir Isaac Newton.

Some readers may be surprised at the variety of scenes depicted on the postcards illustrated. A hundred years ago the humble postcard was the main means of sending a pictorial message of a place or event. Invented in 1894, the picture postcard rapidly became popular and a craze developed for sending them. Every conceivable event and subject was illustrated and the cards were avidly collected in albums. Most towns and villages had their own postcard photographer or publisher eager to satisfy public demand. Forgotten after World War One when radio, telephones and later television provided more instant means of communication, the postcard collections were consigned to the attic. Today old postcards are recognised as unique documents in social history and are once again sought after.

Our tour begins in the south of the district in the famous stone town of Stamford.

Andrew Jenkins
March 2004

All postcards are from the authors' collection.

Front Cover: **Bourne - Market Place.** See page 18 for further information.
Back Cover (top): **Stamford - St. Simon & St. Jude's Fair.** Farmers from a wide area descended on Stamford in November for the traditional two day livestock and produce markets which were held in the town streets. This view shows the cattle market in Broad Street. Notice how the animals are left completely unpenned in the street. The postcard was sent in 1904.
Back Cover (bottom): **Ancaster Quarries.** Ancaster stone is well known throughout the country, many churches in the area are constructed from this honey-coloured limestone. Here workmen are dressing the stone blocks with various picks and chisels. The primitive hand operated gantry crane was used to transport the blocks across the site. Postcard published by T.R. Woolerton c.1904.

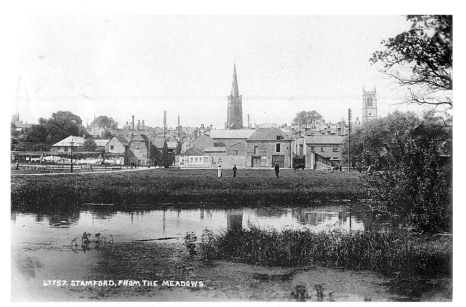

2. Stamford - The Meadows. This is a well known view of the River Welland and The Meadows with All Saints and St. John's churches in the background. Despite its apparent prosperity, Stamford once contained some notorious slum areas. One of these was Cooch's Court seen centre right, now replaced by a car park. Notice the washing hung out along the bank of the Mill Stream, left. A Photochrom Series postcard sent in 1922.

3. Stamford - High Street. It must have been a bright summers day when this Dolby Bros. photograph of the High Street was taken as the shops all have their blinds out, held down by iron weights. St. John's church tower is in the background.

4/5 Uffington. The widespread use of open fires, gas, or candles for lighting and the slow response of horsedrawn fire engines meant that disasterous house fires were relatively commonplace a hundred years ago. Uffington village, a couple of miles east of Stamford, appears to have been particularly unfortunate as the following four cards show. This row of thatched cottages stood on the Stamford road. They burnt down on the 27th June 1910. A large Edwardian villa was built on their site.

6/7 Uffington House was destroyed by fire on December 19th 1904. Architecturally it was one of the best houses in Lincolnshire. Built by the Bertie family (later Earls of Lindsey) in 1688 it had a magnificent interior. Today only the stable block and entrance gates remain. Surprisingly postcards of the fire and ruins are more common than the view before the fire, which was published by Bird & Co. of Stamford.

8. Market Deeping Mill. At one time there were at least seven watermills on the River Welland between Stamford and Market Deeping. At the latter place, this was once a fulling mill used for whitening cloth. Later it became a corn mill. Sadly the mill building was pulled down some years ago. Now only the Mill House on the right remains beside the Stamford road. A Dolby Bros. postcard sent in 1916.

9. Deeping St. James. The River Welland through the Deepings was once busy with barges carrying cargoes as far as Stamford. West of Market Deeping, a canal was built beside the river. Traffic on the canal ended in 1863 due to competition from the railways. The lock seen on this postcard marked the start of the canalised section and its remains can still be seen beside Bridge Street. Postcard published by Dolby Bros. c.1910

10. Market Deeping - Church Street. The village grew up on the coaching trade on the main route from London to Lincoln. Taken from the foot of the bridge over the River Welland, this view looks towards the 13th century St. Guthlac's Church. R. Garratts' Central Supply Stores on the left sold everything from groceries to boots and clothes. Sanderson's Drapers is on the right of the street. Postcard published by Dolby Bros. c.1910.

11. Market Deeping - Towngate. A picture taken around 1905 of the crossroads on the northern edge of the village. The view is hardly recognisable today. Only the George Inn, now a private house, and adjoining building are still standing. The modern Towngate Inn now occupies the field in the distance. Other buildings have long since been removed. Towngate was once the site of a mediaeval fair and the remains of a cross still stand near the junction.

12. **Casewick Hall** is situated down a long drive outside Uffington. It is a handsome Elizabethan house built in 1621 by the Trollope family. The gardens contain many rare plants and trees collected by the 2nd baron Kesteven.

Greatford

13. **Greatford** is a quiet village a few miles north east of Stamford. Many of the cottages once belonged to Greatford Hall. Its owner, Major C.C.L. Fitzwilliam, had sculptured stone crowns and obelisks placed in their gardens, some of which can still be seen. This view published by A Webster of Barnack and posted in 1908 looks west along the village street towards the Hare & Hounds Inn.

14. Greatford Hall was built early in the 16th century by a Calais woolstapler and was noted for its splendid oak fittings. During the late 1700s it was owned by Dr Francis Willis, the physician known for curing King George III of his madness. Tragedy struck on 5th September 1922 when a fire broke out. Water drawn from the stream running through the grounds failed to quell the flames and the hall had to be completely rebuilt. Postcard by G.F. Hinson of Stamford.

15. Holywell Hall. Holywell is a very pretty spot in a small valley. The 17th century hall and church are built close to an iron water spring. The orange colour of the water was likened to blood hence *Holy-Well*. Quarries nearby are said to have supplied the stone used to build Windsor Castle. Another view by G.F. Hinson.

16. Witham-on-the-Hill, south west of Bourne, has the appearance of a typical estate village. Dating back to Saxon times, it was once part of the estate of Hereward the Wake. The Johnson family, founders of Witham Hall, rebuilt these cottages on Little Bytham road after a fire in 1775.

17. Witham-on-the-Hill. Walter Fenwick, a wealthy businessman, bought the Witham estate in 1902. He turned Witham-on-the-Hill into a model village and extended Witham Hall. In 1913 Walters' flamboyant eldest son, Keld, celebrated his 21st birthday with a garden party for the entire village. Here we see a group of the guests outside the Orangery at the Hall. In those days everybody in Witham-on-the-Hill was either employed by or dependent on the estate. The postcard was sent a few days after the event.

18. Witham-on-the-Hill. In 1905 the village pub was moved from its site on Little Bytham Road to this new building, the *Six Bells*, at the opposite end of the village. Apparently this was done on the instructions of the squire, Walter Fenwick, because he disliked the sight and sound of his workers revelling opposite the gates to Witham Hall.

19. The Bowthorpe Oak can be found just east of the Bourne to Stamford road near the village of Manthorpe. With an estimated age of between 700 and 1000 years, it is a contender for the oldest oak in Britain. The tree has a girth of over 15 yards and is hollow within. At one time it contained a circular seat capable of holding 15 people, a roof and a door. Postcard published by Ashby Swift of Bourne, sent in 1906.

20. Toft. Looking up the hill towards Bourne in the village of Toft on the Stamford road. In the background is the *The Bakers' Arms*, which closed many years ago. Notice the couple out for an excursion in the Bourne Ales delivery cart. Postcard sent in 1907.

21. Thurlby. It is thought that this picture of Long Drove, near the village crossroads depicts the celebrations to mark King Edward VII's Coronation in 1902. Thurlby is a typical fen edge village. The Roman canal, the Car Dyke, crosses the road behind the Church Hall in the centre of the picture. Postcard sent in 1905.

22. Graysons Waggon, Northorpe. This farm waggon from Northorpe near Thurlby was typical of those used on the vast fenland fields. An early guide book described the scene: *"Every foot of land is cultivated, neat hedges, clean cut dykes, great fields of corn, huge waggons with three or four enormous shire horses yoked to each".*

THE POND, BASTON. 103.

23. Baston. A view of the long Main Street looking east towards the fen. Quite a mixture of building styles are visible. Church Street is to the right. The village pond, which is looking a bit low in this Dolby Bros. picture, has now been filled in. The postcard was sent in 1925.

Photo by)   BOURNE, from the CHURCH.   (Ashby Swift.

24. Bourne. An interesting panorama over the western part of Bourne taken from the tower of the Abbey Church. South Street runs across the foreground. Some of the sheds seen are part of R.H. Mills' Bourne Mineral Water Co. and the Masons Arms is visible to the right. Behind is the terrace of Wood View. The fields beyond towards Bourne Woods are now covered by modern housing. Postcard published by Ashby Swift c. 1905.

25. Bourne - Town Hall. Ashby Swift produced this unusual photographic Christmas card made from branches and stuffed birds framing a picture of the Market Square. The Town Hall with a curious cut away frontage was designed by Browning of Stamford in 1821. Next door the Bull Inn has been rebuilt and is now the Burghley Arms.

26. **Bourne - The Red Hall** in South Street is a fine Elizabethan mansion originally owned by the Digby family. In 1860 it was used as part of Bourne railway station until the line closed in 1959. The railway buildings seen behind have now gone and the hall is now in a more tranquil setting. Postcard sent in 1914, published by Redshaw Bros.

27. **Bourne Fen Flood.** The low lying fenland to the east of Bourne has always been subject to severe flooding. A breach in the bank of the River Glen occurred in 1910 when many hundreds of acres of land were inundated. This anonymous postcard shows workers attempting to fill the gap with sandbags.

28. Morton, two miles north of Bourne, is a typical fen edge village with a long wide main street. At the east end is the church of St. John the Baptist with its unusually large clock. However this view c1905 by Ashby Swift looks west towards the crossroads with the Sleaford to Bourne road. In the background is the Lord Nelson Inn which has now been completely altered.

29. Morton Station. A few passengers wait at the sleepy Morton Road Station on the Bourne to Sleaford branch line of the Great Northern Railway. The station, down a lane at the east end of the village closed in 1930. The station building is still standing but is now surrounded by modern housing. An Ashby Swift postcard c.1905.

30. Rippingale. The local meet of fox-hounds was quite an event in village life. Here a sizeable crowd have gathered to watch the Belvoir Hounds outside St. Andrews church in Rippingale. This postcard was sent to France in 1908.

31. Grimsthorpe Castle owned by the Willoughby de Eresby family, (Dukes of Ancaster) stands in 3000 acres of parkland, part of which was once the site of Vaudey Abbey. Originally a mediaeval castle, the house was extended and rebuilt several times. The north front seen here was designed by Vanbrugh. It is not known why the crowd are assembled in front of the main door on this postcard sent in 1905.

32. Bourne - Market Place. A reminder of the time when the market was held in t of the town. The photograph has been taken from the first floor of the Nags Hea￼ North Street. Bottom right is the top of the Ostler memorial fountain which was cemetery around 1960. Postcard sent in 1910 and published by Ashby Swift.

uare
ards
the

33. Edenham is an estate village for Grimsthorpe Castle but Roman remains found on the mound occupied by St. Michael's Church indicate much earlier origins. This view is taken from the Bourne end of the village by the bridge over the East Glen or Eden river. The cottages on the right have been replaced by a more modern bungalow. Postcard published by W.H. Redshaw & Son c.1905.

34. Edenham. At the northern end of the village is the Five Bells Inn. It looks like all the village children have been assembled in their best clothes. Perhaps they have been let out from the school opposite to pose for the photographer. The Reverend Charles Kingsley lived in Edenham for a time in the 19th century and wrote *The Water Babies* and *Hereward the Wake* whilst there. Postcard published by W.H. Redshaw & Son c.1905.

35. Edenham Branch Railway. In the 19th century Lord Willoughby of Grimsthorpe Castle had a great interest in the use of steam power on his estate. After the Great Northern Railway from Peterborough to Grantham opened in 1855 he built a private branch line connecting to it. The railway ran from Little Bytham station to Edenham where it ended in a farmyard. Although carrying both passengers and goods, the line was never profitable and closed in 1873. This rare postcard published by The Locomotive Publishing Co. shows the locomotive HAVILAH at Edenham.

HEATHCOTE R?., CASTLE BYTHAM.

36. Castle Bytham. The mound of the 11th century castle still dominates the village of Castle Bytham. In this view published by Baines of Castle Bytham, the village postman and local children pose in front of the sloping village green. This has now been enlarged following the demolition of the cottages seen facing the camera. The postcard was sent in 1910.

37. Little Bytham. A few children enjoy the snow in this bleak wintry scene. The Great Northern London to York railway is carried over the village on a brick viaduct known as the Nine Arches. It was near here in 1937 that *Mallard* reached 126.5 mph braking the speed record for a steam locomotive. This postcard however was sent in 1908.

38. South Witham Station. It would appear that the photographer climbed to the top of a signal pole to get this view of South Witham station on the line between Saxby Junction and Bourne. The railway closed to passengers in 1959 but remained open to serve the sidings seen to the right. These were associated with extensive iron-stone workings in the area. Later quarrying has now obliterated most of this view. Postcard published by Ashby Swift, sent in 1912.

39. North Witham - Church Army Van. It took some time to discover the location of this superb uncaptioned card of a Church Army van. Eventually the picture was placed as having been taken opposite St. Mary's Church in North Witham. The Church Army was an evangelistic movement founded in 1882 by Wilson Carlile. Its aim was to bring the gospels to everybody, especially the less well off. The field in which the van stands now has houses built on it.

40. Witham Common. The hills of south west Lincolnshire are prime fox hunting country. Here the Cottesmore Hunt is seen leaving the woods at Witham Common in 1908. The Great North Road (A1) passes close to this spot which was once known as a haunt of highwaymen.

41. Colsterworth. This is the Colsterworth Methodist children's procession, part of the 1903 Floral Fete, winding its way through the narrow village street past the old Post Office. This was originally part of the Great North Road. In coaching days Colsterworth had several *"excellent inns"* and was a noted posting town where the coach horses were changed. Postcard published by Ashby Swift of Bourne.

WOOLSTHORPE MANOR. THE BIRTHPLACE OF SIR ISAAC NEWTON.

42. Woolsthorpe Manor. Attached to Colsterworth is the small hamlet of Woolsthorpe. Here at the Manor, Sir Isaac Newton was born in 1642. Scribed into plaster on the walls are several interesting drawings and geometric shapes said to have been made by Newton himself. In the garden is the possible descendent of the famous apple tree which inspired him to develop the theory of gravity. Needham Bros. of Grantham published this postcard. c1908.

43. Stainby is near the border with Leicestershire on the road from Colsterworth to Buckminster. In this view looking west, the long closed Blue Dog Inn is seen on the left with St. Peter's church behind. Fifty years ago Stainby was at the centre of extensive ironstone quarries with a network of railways serving the pits. Today the only evidence of this former activity are the sunken field levels in areas where the ore was extracted. A Towne's Series postcard c.1910.

44. Swinstead is a picturesque village connected with the Ancaster Estate of nearby Grimsthorpe Castle. In this Dolby Bros. postcard, the village children are posed around the old market cross with St. Mary's church in the background. Notice the cast iron village pump to the left of the cross and look out for the small child in a push cart made from an old wooden crate.

45. Swayfield. This is the Royal Oak Inn at Swayfield near Corby Glen. Part of the building dates from the 16th century and there is a legend that Cromwell once stayed at *"the old Inn"*. Behind is Swayfield House. In 1588 a beacon was lit at Swayfield, part of a chain across the country to warn of the approach of the Spanish Armada. A Dolby Bros. postcard sent in 1914.

46. Corby Glen. Until the 1930s it was known as plain *Corby*. The second part of the name *Glen* comes from the nearby river and was added to avoid confusion with the Northamptonshire steel town. In this 1904 Ashby Swift view of the market square and cross, the village windmill can be seen in the distance. The Angel Hotel, one of three inns in the square and Smedley's chemists shop are now private houses.

47. Corby Glen. The eastern side of the market place c.1905. The horse drawn timber waggon was known locally as a *drag* and was on its way to Adcocks sawmills in the village. Behind is Willertons stores and their delivery cart. The shop was a grocers, drapers and post office combined. They also published postcards. A sheep fair has been held annually in the village since 1238.

48. Irnham. This postcard, sent in 1909, was taken outside the Griffin Inn and probably commemorates Irnham Feast Day organised by the Griffin Friendly Society. According to one account, the day started with a procession headed by a brass band. There was then a meal for the villagers at the inn before an afternoon spent *"in harmony with grand music and singing"*. After tea at Irnham Hall there were more speeches and songs late into the evening.

49. Ingoldsby, between Corby Glen and Folkingham, was formerly known for its point to point horse races. The village windmill can be seen in the centre of this photograph taken from the church tower. The wooden mill was of a type known as a post mill; the whole housing rotated around a large post. It was pulled down before 1920. The postcard was published by Ashby Swift of Bourne.

50. Sempringham Church. St. Andrew's Church stands alone in the fields south of Billingborough. It is all that remains of Sempringham Priory where in 1083 St. Gilbert founded the only English monastic order, the Gilbertines. The Abbey was dissolved in 1538 and along with the nearby village, it has completely disappeared. This postcard was posted in 1905.

St. Andrews. Church. Horbling

51. Horbling. A delightful period view taken around 1905 in the village of Horbling just north of Billingborough. St. Andrew's church is in the background. Nobody appears to be attending to the horse and trap in the foreground - perhaps it belonged to the photographer, Mr Owston, who lived in the village.

Folkingham

52. Folkingham. Looking down the distinctively wide market place in Folkingham from outside the Greyhound Inn. This former market town was extensively rebuilt in the 18th century by the Heathcote family, owners of the estate. On the left is The Five Bells Commercial Inn owned by J.T. Hind. This is now a residential home. Postcard sent in 1904.

53. House of Correction, Folkingham. This is the ornate portico to Folkingham House of Correction which was built on the site of the castle bailey in 1808. Behind are the cell blocks, now demolished. The jail closed in 1878 but the portico has been preserved. Note how the postcard uses the old spelling of the village - *Falkingham*. An Ashby Swift postcard sent in 1909.

54. Folkingham Manor House was built in 1616 for Lord Edward Clinton using stone from the ruins of Sempringham Priory and Folkingham Castle. However, when Daniel Defoe visited the manor in the 1720s it had become dilapidated. Now fully restored, it is a prominent feature in the Market Place. Postcard published by Ashby Swift c.1910.

55. C. A. Simpson's Carriers Cart, Grantham. At the turn of the last century, goods were delivered to rural communities by horse drawn carriers waggons. These often took passengers as well, the waggons running to a timetable between local Inns. Simpson's waggon was based at Folkingham and is seen here on St. Peter's Hill in Grantham ready for a return run.

56. Easton Hall, overlooking the river Witham just north of Colsterworth, was started by Henry Cholmeley in 1592 and extended and altered several times. Many famous people visited Easton including Franklin D. Roosevelt, who spent part of his honeymoon here in 1905 around the time this picture was taken. The Hall was demolished shortly after World War II but the overgrown walled gardens are now being restored. A Valentines Series postcard sent in 1909.

WOOLSTHORPE BY BELVOIR.

57. Woolsthorpe by Belvoir. The delivery cart of E. Phillips of Bottesford had just arrived on the small village green when this photograph by Needham Bros. of Grantham was taken. Situated on the western edge of the county, Woolsthorpe is an estate village for Belvoir Castle just over the border in Leicestershire.

HARLAXTON GRANTHAM.

W.R.C. WHEELER
GRANTHAM.

58. Harlaxton. A 1909 postcard by W.R.C. Wheeler of the old cross and High Street. The village contains many curiously designed red brick cottages. These were the work of Gregory Gregory, the builder of Harlaxton Manor, a spectacular Baroque-style mansion completed in the 1830s.

59. Harlaxton Wharf - Grantham Canal. A pair of narrow boats *William* and *Hannah* lie moored at the little wharf serving Harlaxton village. The canal linked Grantham and the River Trent at Nottingham. It was officially abandoned in 1929, however, there are now plans to restore the navigation. The postcard was sent in 1905.

60. Grantham - The Bee Hive. In this view along Castlegate are two of ' Grantham's best known landmarks. In the foreground is the Beehive Inn with its 'living sign' - a tree containing a beehive complete with bees. The spire in the background is of St. Wulframs' Church and rises to 285 feet, one of the highest in the country. A Valentines Series postcard c1912.

WHALEBONE ARCH, NEAR GRANTHAM

61. Great Ponton - The Whalebone Arch. The name *Whalebone Lane* is the only reminder of this arch made from a whale's jawbone at Great Ponton near Grantham. During the 19th century several arches were built from skeletons of whales stranded on the east coast. Locally, the only surviving examples are at Threekingham and Long Sutton. A Valentines Series postcard sent in 1917.

May Parade,
Grantham.
1906.

62. Grantham - May Parade. A variety of decorated horsedrawn carts and waggons assemble in the Market Place before the 1906 May Day parade. The appearance of this square has changed little since the photograph was taken. The postcard was published by Needham Bros.

BLAND'S BUS SERVICES, GRANTHAM.　　Phone 70

PHOTO OF PART OF OUR FLEET OF PULLMAN COACHES. FINEST COACHES AND LOWEST PRICES IN THE DISTRICT. FITTED WITH 4-WHEEL BRAKES & GIANT PNEUMATIC TYRES.

63. Grantham - Westgate. This publicity card probably dates from the late 1920s and shows eight of Bland's coaches lined up in Westgate. Notice how the company proudly proclaim that their coaches are fitted with 4 wheel brakes and pneumatic tyres.

BELTON, Nᴿ GRANTHAM.

W.R.C.WHEELER.
GRANTHAM.

64. Belton. A couple of miles north of Grantham is best known for Belton House, built in the 17th century for the Brownlow family. The village was also owned by the estate and contains many interesting buildings designed by the architect, Salvin. This view by W R C Wheeler of Grantham shows the old village school. The group of women are probably inhabitants of the almshouses to the right.

LONDONTHORPE, Nᴿ GRANTHAM.

W.R.C.WHEELER.
GRANTHAM.

65. Londonthorpe is another Belton estate village situated on a ridge above Grantham. All the women and children of the village appear to have turned out for this photograph taken near the village chapel. Postcard published by W R C Wheeler c1905.